T0401406

ACKNOWLEDGMENTS

Publishing Director	Piers Pickard
Publisher	Tim Cook
Commissioning Editors	Jen Feroze
	Catharine Robertson
Illustrators	Andy Mansfield
	Sebastien Iwohn
Designer	Andy Mansfield
Print production	Larissa Frost,
	Nigel Longuet
With thanks to:	Jennifer Dixon

Published in June 2017 by Lonely Planet Global Ltd
CRN: 554153
ISBN: 978 1 78701 279 0
www.lonelyplanetkids.com
© Lonely Planet 2017
Printed in China

10 9 8 7 6 5 4 3 2 1

Lonely Planet Offices

AUSTRALIA
The Malt Store, Level 3, 551 Swanston St, Carlton, Victoria 3053
T: 03 8379 8000

IRELAND
Unit E, Digital Court, The Digital Hub,
Rainsford St, Dublin 8

USA
124 Linden St, Oakland, CA 94607
T: 510 250 6400

UK
240 Blackfriars Rd, London SE1 8NW
T: 020 3771 5100

STAY IN TOUCH lonelyplanet.com/contact

first words
ENGLISH

Illustrated by
Andy Mansfield & Sebastien Iwohn

hello

(huh-loh)

ice cream

(eye-skreem)

water

(wah-tur)

supermarket

(soo-pur-mar-kit)

shopping cart
(shah-ping kart)

cat

(kat)

bus

(buss)

dress

(dress)

dog

(dahg)

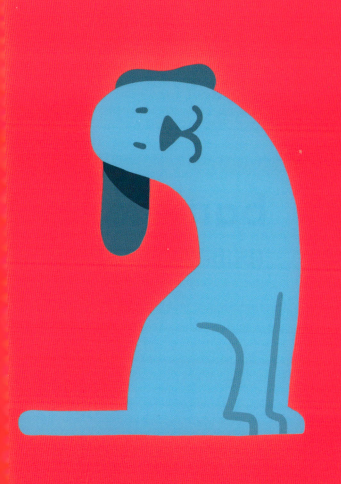

banana

(buh-na-nuh)

carrot

(ka-rut)

taxi

(tak-see)

t-shirt

(tee-shurt)

fish

(fish)

airplane

(air-plane)

horse

(horss)

french fries

(frentch fryz)

swimming pool

(swim-ing pool)

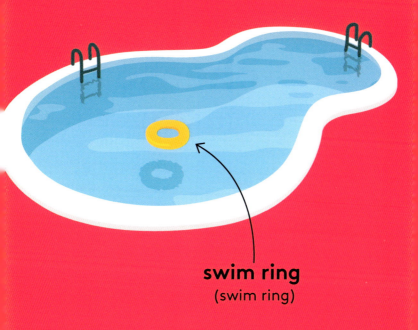

swim ring

(swim ring)

cheese

(tcheez)

towel

(tao-ul)

doctor

(dahk-tur)

apple
(a-pul)

worm
(wurm)

beach

(beetch)

bicycle

(by-si-kul)

airport

(air-port)

juice

(jooss)

bakery

(bay-kuh-ree)

shoes

(shooz)

phone

(fone)

post office

(pohst off-iss)

restaurant

(ress-tuh-rahnt)

hotel

(hoh-tel)

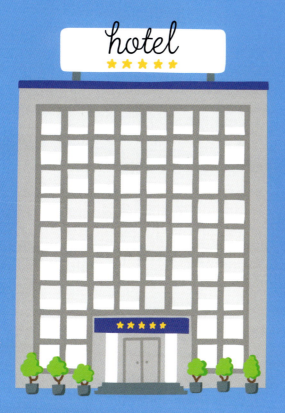

milk

(milk)

chocolate

(chahk-let)

car

(kar)

hat

(hat)

sunglasses

(sun-glass-iz)

chicken

(tchik-in)

train

(trane)

station

(stay-shun)

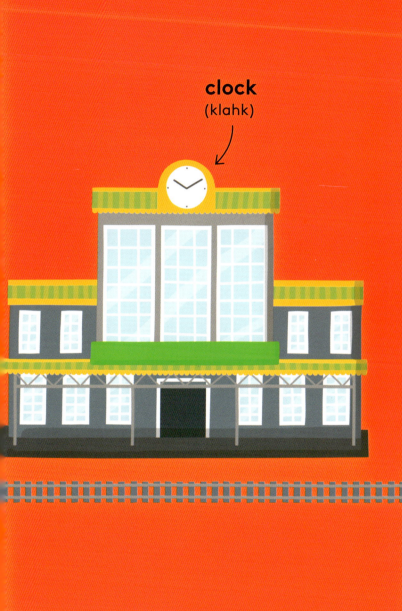

toilet

(toy-let)

bed

(bed)

house

(houss)

chimney
(chim-nee)

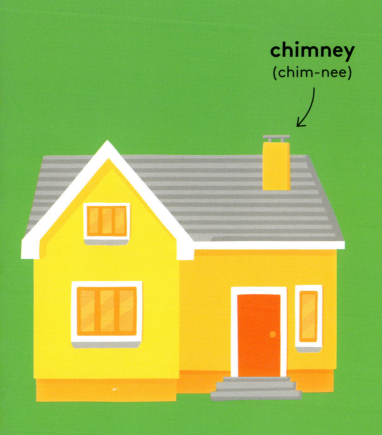

pants

(pants)

suitcase

(soot-kayss)

plate

(playt)

knife

(nife)

fork

(fork)

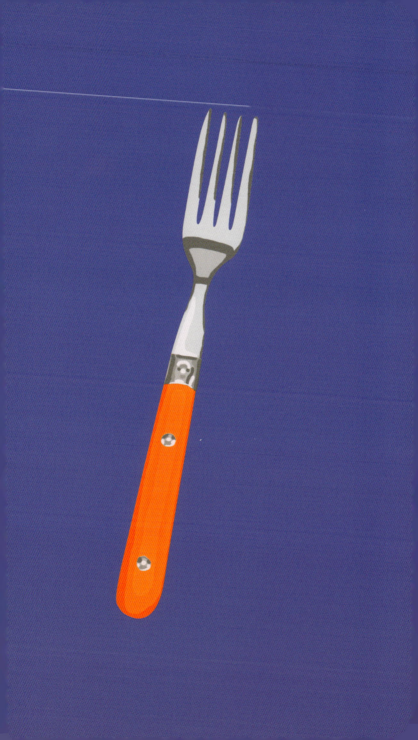

spoon

(spoon)

computer

(kum-pyoo-tur)

mouse
(mouss)

book

(book)

sandwich

(sand-witch)

yes

(yess)

no

(noh)

movie theater

(moo-vee thee-uh-tur)

park

(park)

menu

(men-yoo)

passport

(pass-port)

police officer

(puh-leess off-uh-sur)

key
(kee)

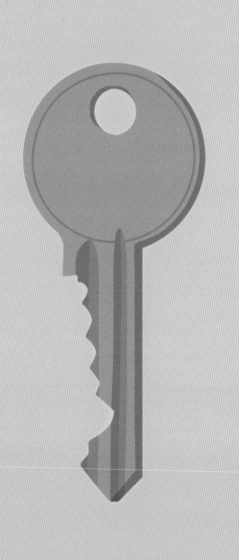

ticket

(tik-it)

pineapple
(pine-ap-ul)

rain

(rayn)

snow

(snoh)

sun

(sun)

tree

(tree)

flower

(flao-ur)

cake

(kayk)

cherry
(tche-ree)

ball

(bawl)

bird

(burd)

egg

(eg)

umbrella

(um-brel-uh)

rabbit

(rab-it)

money

(muh-nee)

bank

(bank)

mouse

(mouss)

scarf

(skarf)

gloves

(gluhvs)

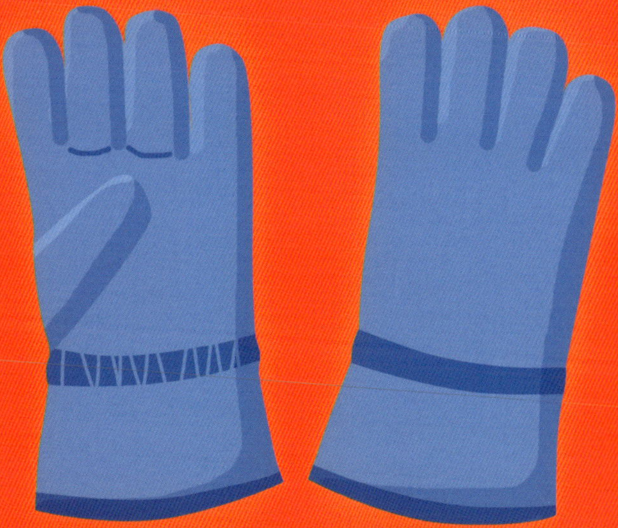

coat

(kote)

hospital

(hah-spi-tul)

chair

(tchair)

table

(tay-bul)

toothbrush

(tooth-brush)

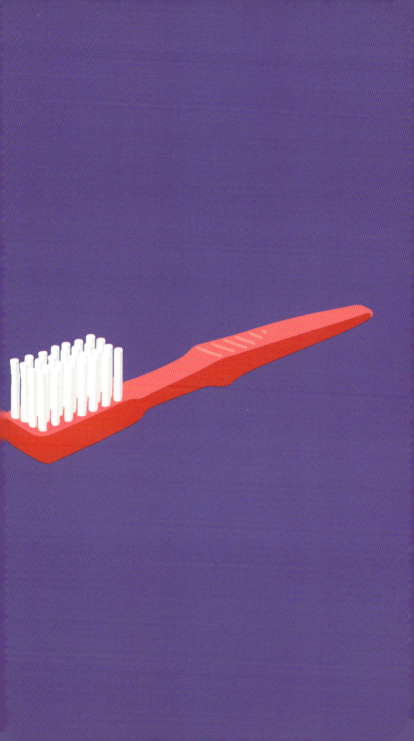

toothpaste

(tooth-payst)

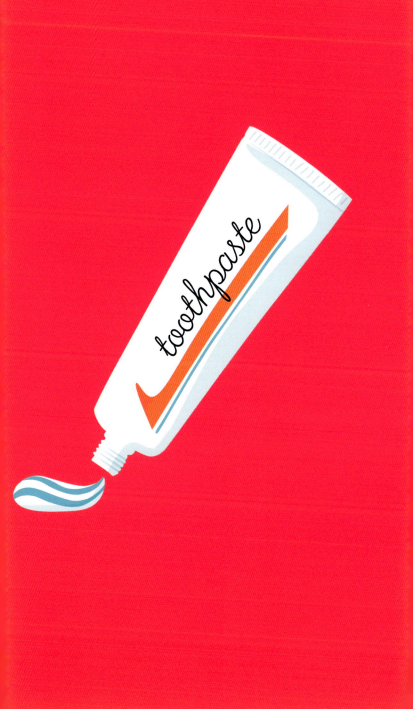

sunscreen

(sun-skreen)

lion

(lye-un)

elephant

(el-uh-funt)

monkey

(mung-kee)

spider

(spy-dur)

burger

(bur-gur)

pen

(pen)

door

(dor)

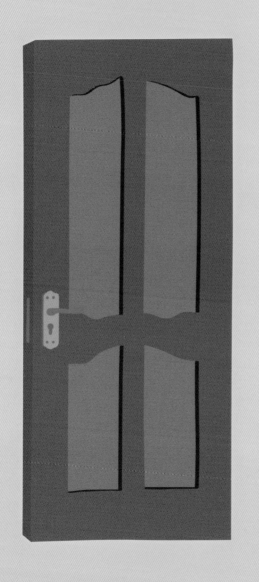

window

(win-doh)

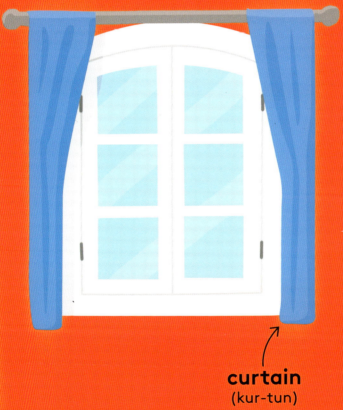

curtain
(kur-tun)

tent

(tent)

church

(tchurtch)

tomato

(tuh-may-toh)

moon

(moon)

stars

(starz)

postcard

(pohst-kard)

stamp
(stamp)

boat

(bote)

goodbye

(good-by)